D0967700

PRAYERS

of a

Loving
Mother

PRAYERS

of a

Loving Mother

THIRD EDITION

Cover design & page layout by: Bart Dawson
Copy written and compiled by: Criswell Freeman

ISBN 1-58334-212-5
      1 2 3 4 5 6 7 8 9 10 • 03 04 05 06 07 08 09 10

Printed in the United States of America

Contents

A Prayer for . . .

Introduction

In your hands, you hold a book entitled *Prayers of a Loving Mother*. Perhaps you received this book as a gift from your child or husband. Or, perhaps, amid the hustle and bustle of your busy life, you picked up this book of your own accord. Either way, you will be blessed if you take the words on these pages to heart.

Life is a fabric of habits, woven together—thread by thread—by the countless, largely unremembered actions that make up the entirety of our days. Our habits determine, in large part, who we are and who we become. If we develop habits that enrich our lives and the lives of others, we are blessed by God. If, on the other hand, we fall prey to negative thoughts or destructive behaviors, we suffer.

No habit is more important to your daily life than the habit of regular prayer and worship. This book is intended to assist you in your daily devotional readings. As such, this text is divided into 31 chapters, one for each day of the month. Each chapter contains Bible verses, a brief essay, inspirational quotations from noted Christian thinkers, and a prayer.

During the next 31 days, please try this experiment: read a chapter each day. If you're already committed to a daily time of worship, this book will enrich that experience. If you are not, the simple act of giving God a few minutes each morning will change the tone and direction of your life.

Every day provides opportunities to put God where He belongs: at the center of your life. When you do so, you will worship your Creator, not just with words but also with deeds. And then, just as He has promised, God will smile upon you, upon your family, and upon generations yet unborn.

Day 1
A Prayer for . . .
God's Grace

For it is by grace you have been saved,
through faith—and this not from yourselves,
it is the gift of God—not by works,
so that no one can boast.

Ephesians 2:8-9 NIV

As a mother, you know the profound love that you hold in your heart for your own children. As a child of God, you can only imagine the infinite love that your Heavenly Father holds for you.

God made you in His own image and gave you salvation through the person of His Son Jesus Christ. And now, precisely because you are a wondrous creation treasured by God, a question presents itself: What will you do in response to the Creator's love? Will you ignore it or embrace it? Will you return it or neglect it? That decision, of course, is yours and yours alone.

When you embrace God's love, you are forever changed. When you embrace God's love, you feel differently about yourself, your neighbors, your family, and your world. More importantly, you share God's message—and His love—with others.

Your Heavenly Father—a God of infinite love and mercy—is waiting to embrace you with open arms. Accept His love today and forever.

The cross was heavy, the blood was real,
and the price was extravagant. It would have
bankrupted you or me, so He paid it for us.
Call it simple. Call it a gift. But don't call it
easy. Call it what it is. Call it grace.

Max Lucado

~

Grace: a gift that costs everything for
the giver and nothing for the recipient.

Philip Yancey

~

In your greatest weakness, turn to your greatest
strength, Jesus, and hear Him say,
"My grace is sufficient for you, for
My strength is made perfect in weakness"
(2 Corinthians 12:9, NKJV).

Lisa Whelchel

~

The grace of God transcends all our feeble
efforts to describe it. It cannot be poured into
any mental receptacle without running over.

Vance Havner

Dear Lord, You have offered Your grace freely
through Christ Jesus. I praise You for
that priceless gift. Let me share the Good News
of Your Son with a world that desperately
needs His peace, His abundance,
His love, and His salvation.
~ Amen

My Prayer for Today

Day 2

A Prayer for . . .

Our Families

Choose for yourselves this day whom you
will serve . . . as for me and my household,
we will serve the LORD.

Joshua 24:15 NIV

As every mother knows, family life is a mixture of conversations, mediations, irritations, deliberations, commiserations, frustrations, negotiations, and celebrations. In other words, the life of the typical mom is incredibly varied.

Certainly, in the life of every family, there are moments of frustration and disappointment. Lots of them. But, for those who are lucky enough to live in the presence of a close-knit, caring clan, the rewards far outweigh the frustrations.

No family is perfect, and neither is yours. But, despite the inevitable challenges and occasional hurt feelings of family life, your clan is God's gift to you. That little band of men, women, kids, and babies is a priceless treasure on temporary loan from the Father above. Give thanks to the Giver for the gift of family . . . and act accordingly.

We must strengthen our commitment to
model strong families ourselves, to live by
godly priorities in a culture where self so often
supersedes commitment to others. And, as we
not only model but assertively reach out to help
others, we must realize that even huge societal
problems are solved one person at a time.

Chuck Colson

~

A home is a place where we find direction.

Gigi Graham Tchividjian

~

The only true source of meaning in life is found
in love for God and His Son Jesus Christ,
and love for mankind, beginning
with our own families.

James Dobson

~

The first essential for a happy home is love.

Billy Graham

A Prayer for Today

Dear Lord, You have blessed me with
a family to love and to care for. Protect
my family, Lord. And, let me show them
love and acceptance, so that through me
they might come to know You.

~ Amen

My Prayer for Today

Day 3

A Prayer for . . .

God's Strength

Do you not know? Have you not heard?
The Everlasting God, the LORD, the Creator of
the ends of the earth does not become weary
or tired. His understanding is inscrutable. He gives
strength to the weary, and to him who lacks might
He increases power. Though youths grow weary
and tired, and vigorous young men stumble badly,
yet those who wait for the LORD will gain new
strength; they will mount up with wings like eagles,
they will run and not get tired, they will walk
and not become weary.

Isaiah 40:28-31 NASB

I f you're a mother with too many demands and too few hours in which to meet them, you are not alone. Motherhood is perhaps the world's most demanding profession. But don't fret: even when it seems that your responsibilities are simply too great to bear, you and God, working together, can handle them. So focus, not upon the difficulties of your circumstances but, instead, upon God and upon His love for you. Then, ask Him for the strength that you need to fulfill your daily duties.

When you turn your thoughts and prayers to your Heavenly Father, He will give you the energy and the perspective to complete the most important items on your to-do list. And then, once you've done your best, leave the rest up to God. He can handle it . . . and will.

God walks with us. He scoops us up in
His arms or simply sits with us in silent
strength until we cannot avoid the awesome
recognition that yes, even now, He is here.

Gloria Gaither

~

Notice what Jesus had to say concerning those
who have wearied themselves by trying to do
things in their own strength: "Come to me,
all you who labor and are heavy laden,
and I will give you rest."

Henry Blackaby and Claude King

~

God is the One who provides our strength,
not only to cope with the demands of the day
but also to rise above them. May we look to
Him for the strength to soar.

Jim Gallery

~

Measure the size of the obstacles
against the size of God.

Beth Moore

Dear Lord, being a mother isn't easy.
Sometimes, I am worried; sometimes, I am
weary; and sometimes, I become discouraged.
When I am worried, give me faith. When my
responsibilities seem overwhelming, give me
strength and perspective. And keep me mindful,
Lord, that You are the ultimate source of my
hope, my strength, my peace, and my salvation.
~ Amen

My Prayer for Today

A Prayer for . . .

Wisdom

Trust in the LORD with all thine heart;
and lean not unto thine own understanding.
In all thy ways acknowledge him,
and he shall direct thy paths.

Proverbs 3:5-6 KJV

Do you seek wisdom for yourself and for your family? Of course you do. But as a savvy mom, you know that wisdom can be an elusive commodity in today's troubled world. In a society filled with temptations and distractions, it's easy for parents and children alike to stray far from the source of the ultimate wisdom: God's Holy Word.

When you begin a daily study of God's Word and live according to His commandments, you will become wise . . . in time. But don't expect to open your Bible today and be wise tomorrow. Wisdom is not like a mushroom; it does not spring up overnight. It is, instead, like an oak tree that starts as a tiny acorn, grows into a sapling, and eventually reaches up to the sky, tall and strong.

Today and every day, study God's Word and live by it. In time, you will accumulate a storehouse of wisdom that will enrich your own life and the lives of your family members, your friends, and the world.

The person who prays ceases to be a fool.

Oswald Chambers

~

If you lack knowledge, go to school.
If you lack wisdom, get on your knees.

Vance Havner

~

Knowledge can be found in books or in school.
Wisdom, on the other hand,
starts with God . . . and ends there.

Marie T. Freeman

~

For the Lord gives wisdom, and from his mouth
come knowledge and understanding.

Proverbs 2:6 NIV

Dear Lord, give me wisdom to love my family,
to care for them, to teach them, and to lead
them. Make me wise in Your ways and in
Your Holy Word. Let me share Your wisdom
through words and deeds, today
and every day that I live.
~ Amen

My Prayer for Today

Day 5

A Prayer for . . .

Today

This is the day which the LORD has made;
let us rejoice and be glad in it.

Psalm 118:24 NASB

What do you expect from the day ahead? Are you expecting God to do wonderful things, or are you living beneath a cloud of apprehension and doubt? The familiar words of Psalm 118:24 remind us of a profound yet simple truth: God made this day and gave it to us as a gift. We, in response to that gift, should be grateful.

For Christian believers, every day begins and ends with God and His Son. Christ came to this earth to give us abundant life and eternal salvation. We give thanks to our Maker when we treasure each day and use it to the fullest.

Today, let us give thanks for the gift of life and for the One who created it. And then, let's use this day—a precious gift from the Father above—to serve our Savior faithfully, courageously, and joyfully.

Wherever you are, be all there.
Live to the hilt every situation you
believe to be the will of God.

Jim Elliot

～

Today is mine. Tomorrow is none of
my business. If I peer anxiously into the fog of
the future, I will strain my spiritual eyes so
that I will not see clearly what is
required of me now.

Elisabeth Elliot

～

Now is the only time worth having because,
indeed, it is the only time we have.

C. H. Spurgeon

～

Jesus intended for us to be overwhelmed by
the blessings of regular days. He said it was
the reason He had come: "I am come that they
might have life, and that they might have it
more abundantly."

Gloria Gaither

Lord, You have given me another day of life;
let me celebrate this day, and let me use it
according to Your plan. I praise You, Father,
for my life and for the friends and family
members who make it rich. Enable me to live
each moment to the fullest as I give thanks
for Your creation, for Your love,
and for Your Son.

~ Amen

My Prayer for Today

A Prayer for . . .

Righteousness

For the eyes of the Lord are over the righteous,
and his ears are open unto their prayers:
but the face of the Lord is against them
that do evil.

1 Peter 3:12 KJV

God has given us a guidebook for righteous living called the Holy Bible. It contains thorough instructions that, if followed, lead to fulfillment, righteousness, and salvation. But, if we choose to ignore God's commandments, the results are as predictable as they are tragic.

The Bible instructs us that a righteous life has many components: faith, honesty, generosity, love, kindness, humility, gratitude, and worship, to name but a few. And, if we seek to follow the steps of our Savior, Jesus Christ, we must, to the best of our abilities, live according to the principles contained in God's Holy Word.

As a loving mother, you are keenly aware that God has entrusted you with a profound responsibility: caring for the needs of your family, including their spiritual needs. To fulfill that responsibility, you must study God's Word and live by it. When you do, your example will be a blessing not only to your loved ones but also to generations yet unborn.

Our souls were made to live in an upper atmosphere, and we stifle and choke if we live on any lower level. Our eyes were made to look off from these heavenly heights, and our vision is distorted by any lower gazing.

Hannah Whitall Smith

∽

What is God looking for? He is looking for men and women whose hearts are completely His.

Charles Swindoll

∽

Blessed are those who hunger and thirst for righteousness, for they will be filled.

Matthew 5:6 NIV

∽

A life growing in its purity and devotion will be a more prayerful life.

E. M. Bounds

A Prayer for Today

Lord, my family is both a priceless gift
and a profound responsibility. Let my actions
be worthy of that responsibility. Lead me along
Your path, Lord, and guide me far from
the frustrations and distractions of this troubled
world. Let Your Holy Word guide my actions,
and let Your love reside in my heart,
this day and every day.

~ Amen

My Prayer for Today

A Prayer for . . .

The Power to Encourage

So then we pursue the things which make
for peace and the building up of one another.

Romans 14:19 NASB

Every member of your family needs a regular supply of encouraging words and pats on the back. And you need the rewards that God gives to enthusiastic moms who are a continual source of encouragement to their families.

In his letter to the Ephesians, Paul writes, "Do not let any unwholesome talk come out of your mouths, but only what is helpful for building others up according to their needs, that it may benefit those who listen" (v. 29 NIV). This passage reminds us that, as Christians, we are instructed to choose our words carefully so as to build others up through wholesome, honest encouragement. How can we build others up? By celebrating their victories and their accomplishments. As the old saying goes, "When someone does something good, applaud—you'll make two people happy."

Today, look for the good in others—starting with your family. And then, celebrate the good that you find. When you do, you'll be a powerful force of encouragement in your corner of the world . . . and a worthy servant to your God.

We urgently need people who encourage
and inspire us to move toward God and away
from the world's enticing pleasures.

Jim Cymbala

~

Encouragement is the oxygen of the soul.

John Maxwell

~

Words. Do you fully understand their power?
Can any of us really grasp the mighty force
behind the things we say? Do we stop
and think before we speak, considering
the potency of the words we utter?

Joni Eareckson Tada

~

A lot of people have gone further than
they thought they could because
someone else thought they could.

Zig Ziglar

Dear Lord, let me be a source of encouragement
to my family. Just as You have lifted me up,
let me also lift up my loved ones so that they
may use their gifts for the glory
of Your kingdom.

~ Amen

My Prayer for Today

My Hopes & Prayers for Next Week

My Hopes & Prayers for Next Week

Day 8
A Prayer for . . .
God's Blessings

For surely, O LORD, you bless the righteous;
you surround them with your favor as with a shield.

Psalm 5:12 NIV

Have you counted your blessings lately? You should. Of course, God's gifts are too numerous to count, but as a grateful Christian mother, you should attempt to count them nonetheless.

Your blessings include life, family, friends, talents, and possessions, for starters. And your greatest gift—a treasure that was paid for on the cross and is yours for the asking—is God's gift of salvation through Christ Jesus.

As believing Christians, we have all been blessed beyond measure. Thus, thanksgiving should become a habit, a regular part of our daily routines. Today, let us pause and thank our Creator for His blessings. And, let us demonstrate our gratitude to the Giver of all things good by using His gifts for the glory of His kingdom.

God is more anxious to bestow His blessings
on us than we are to receive them.

St. Augustine

~

Oh! what a Savior, gracious to all,
Oh! how His blessings round us fall,
Gently to comfort, kindly to cheer,
Sleeping or waking, God is near.

Fanny Crosby

~

We do not need to beg Him to bless us;
He simply cannot help it.

Hannah Whitall Smith

~

Think of the blessings we so easily take for
granted: Life itself; preservation from danger;
every bit of health we enjoy; every hour of
liberty; the ability to see, to hear, to speak,
to think, and to imagine all this
comes from the hand of God.

Billy Graham

A Prayer for Today

Lord, You have given me so much,
and I am thankful. Today, I seek Your blessings
for my family and for myself. Let us use
Your gifts by sharing them with others.
And when we do so, may the glory be Yours.
~ Amen

My Prayer for Today

A Prayer for . . .

The Wisdom to Forgive

Blessed are the merciful,
for they will be shown mercy.

Matthew 5:7 NIV

Even the most mild-mannered moms will, on occasion, have reason to become angry with the inevitable shortcomings of family members and friends. But wise women are quick to forgive others, just as God has forgiven them.

Forgiveness is God's commandment, but oh how difficult a commandment it can be to follow. Being frail, fallible, imperfect human beings, we are quick to anger, quick to blame, slow to forgive, and even slower to forget. No matter. Even when forgiveness is difficult, God's Word is clear.

If, in your heart, you hold bitterness against even a single person, forgive. If there exists even one person, alive or dead, whom you have not forgiven, follow God's commandment and His will for your life: forgive. If you are embittered against yourself for some past mistake or shortcoming, forgive. Then, to the best of your abilities, forget, and move on. Bitterness and regret are not part of God's plan for your life. Forgiveness is.

To be a Christian means to forgive
the inexcusable, because God has forgiven
the inexcusable in you.

C. S. Lewis

~

Our relationships with other people are of
primary importance to God. Because God is
love, He cannot tolerate any unforgiveness
or hardness in us toward any individual.

Catherine Marshall

~

Forgiveness is actually the best revenge
because it not only sets us free from
the person we forgive, but it frees us to move
into all that God has in store for us.

Stormie Omartian

~

Forgiveness is the key that unlocks the door
of resentment and the handcuffs of hate.
It is a power that breaks the chains of
bitterness and the shackles of selfishness.

Corrie ten Boom

A Prayer for Today

Dear Lord, when I am bitter, You can change
my unforgiving heart. And, when I am slow
to forgive, Your Word reminds me that
forgiveness is Your commandment.
Let me be Your obedient servant, Lord,
and let me forgive others
just as You have forgiven me.
~ Amen

My Prayer for Today

A Prayer for . . .

The Courage to Trust

In God, whose word I praise,
in God I trust; I will not be afraid.

Psalm 56:4 NIV

Open your Bible to its center, and you'll find the Book of Psalms. In it are some of the most beautiful words ever translated into the English language, with none more beautiful than the 23rd Psalm. David describes God as being like a shepherd who cares for His flock. No wonder these verses have provided comfort and hope for generations of believers.

You are precious in the eyes of God. You are His priceless creation, made in His image, and protected by Him. God watches over every step you make and every breath you take, so you need never be afraid. But sometimes, fear has a way of slipping into the minds and hearts of even the most devout believers. You are no exception.

On occasion, you will confront circumstances that trouble you to the very core of your soul. When you are afraid, trust in God. When you are worried, turn your concerns over to Him. When you are anxious, be still and listen for the quiet assurance of God's promises. And then, place your life in His hands. He is your shepherd today and throughout eternity. Trust the Shepherd.

God is God. He knows what He is doing.
When you can't trace His hand, trust His heart.

Max Lucado

~

As God's children, we are the recipients of
lavish love—a love that motivates us to
keep trusting even when we have no idea
what God is doing.

Beth Moore

~

Trust in yourself and you are doomed to
disappointment; trust in money and you may
have it taken from you, but trust in God,
and you are never to be confounded
in time or eternity.

D. L. Moody

Lord, when I trust in the things of this earth,
I will be disappointed. But, when I put
my faith in You, I am secure. In every
aspect of my life, Lord, let me trust in
Your boundless grace . . .
today, tomorrow, and forever.
~ Amen

My Prayer for Today

Day 11

A Prayer for . . .

God's Presence

Be still, and know that I am God . . . .

Psalm 46:10 KJV

If you are a busy mother with more obligations than you have time to count, you know all too well that the demands of everyday life can, on occasion, seem overwhelming. Thankfully, even on the days when you feel overburdened, overworked, overstressed and under-appreciated, God is trying to get His message through . . . your job is to listen.

Are you tired, discouraged, or fearful? Be comforted because God is with you. Are you confused? Listen to the quiet voice of your Heavenly Father. Are you bitter? Talk with God and seek His guidance. In whatever condition you find yourself—whether you are happy or sad, victorious or vanquished, troubled or triumphant—carve out moments of silent solitude to celebrate God's gifts and to experience His presence.

The familiar words of Psalm 46:10 remind us to be still before the Creator. When we do, we encounter the awesome presence of our loving Heavenly Father, and we are comforted in the knowledge that God is not just near. He is here.

Our battles are first won or lost in the secret
places of our will in God's presence,
never in full view of the world.

Oswald Chambers

~

Be strong and courageous. Do not be terrified;
do not be discouraged, for the LORD your God
will be with you wherever you go.

Joshua 1:9 NIV

~

Where can I go from your Spirit? Where can
I flee from your presence? If I go up to the
heavens, you are there; if I make my bed in
the depths, you are there. If I rise on the wings
of the dawn, if I settle on the far side of the sea,
even there your hand will guide me,
your right hand will hold me fast.

Psalm 139:7-10 NIV

~

It is God to whom and with whom we travel,
and while He is the End of our journey,
He is also at every stopping place.

Elisabeth Elliot

A Prayer for Today

Slow me down, Lord, so that I might feel Your
presence and Your peace. When the demands
of the day begin to press down upon me,
let me turn to You for strength. When I am
hurried, angered, embittered, or discouraged,
keep me mindful of Your blessings,
Your commandments, Your mercy,
and Your Son.
~ Amen

My Prayer for Today

A Prayer for . . .

A Generous Heart

God has given gifts to each of you from
his great variety of spiritual gifts. Manage them well
so that God's generosity can flow through you.

1 Peter 4:10 NLT

A Prayer for . . .

Hymn writer Fanny Crosby wrote, "To God be the glory; great things He hath done! So loved He the world that He gave us His Son." God's love for us is so complete that He sent Jesus to this earth so that we, His believers, might have eternal life: "But God demonstrates his own love for us in this: While we were still sinners, Christ died for us" (Romans 5:8 NIV).

We, as Christ's followers, are challenged to share His love. We do so, in part, by dealing generously and lovingly with others.

When we walk each day with Christ—and obey the commandments found in God's Holy Word—we are worthy ambassadors for Him. Just as Christ has been—and will always be—the ultimate friend to His flock, so should we be Christlike in the love and generosity we show to those in need. When we give of ourselves and of our possessions—and when we do so cheerfully and humbly—we share a priceless gift: the love of Christ. May we share it today and every day that we live.

I have held many things in my hands,
and I have lost them all; but whatever I have
placed in God's hands, that I still possess.

Martin Luther

~

In the kingdom of God, the surest way to lose
something is to try to protect it,
and the best way to keep it is to let it go.

A. W. Tozer

~

The measure of a life, after all,
is not its duration but its donation.

Corrie ten Boom

~

Abundant living means abundant giving.

E. Stanley Jones

A Prayer for Today

Dear Lord, You have been so generous with me;
let me be generous with others. Help me to be
generous with my time and my possessions as
I care for those in need. Help me to teach
my children to be cheerful givers, Father,
and make us all humble givers, so that
the glory and the praise might be Yours.

~ Amen

My Prayer for Today

Day 13

A Prayer for . . .

Contentment

I have learned to be content
whatever the circumstances.

Philippians 4:11 NIV

A Prayer for . . .

Where can we find contentment? Is it a result of wealth or power or beauty or fame? Hardly. Genuine contentment is a gift from God to those who trust Him and follow His commandments.

Our modern world seems preoccupied with the search for happiness. We are bombarded with messages telling us that happiness depends upon the acquisition of material possessions. These messages are false. Enduring peace is not the result of our acquisitions; it is a spiritual gift from God to those who obey Him and accept His will.

If we don't find contentment in God, we will never find it anywhere else. But, if we seek Him and obey Him, we will be blessed with an inner peace that is beyond human understanding. When God dwells at the center of our lives, peace and contentment will belong to us just as surely as we belong to God.

If we know we have pleased God,
contentment will be our consolation,
for what pleases God will please us.

Kay Arthur

~

Contentment is not escape from battle,
but rather an abiding peace and confidence
in the midst of battle.

Warren Wiersbe

~

Oh, what a happy soul I am, although
I cannot see! I am resolved that in this world,
contented I will be.

Fanny Crosby

~

We will never be happy until we make God
the source of our fulfillment
and the answer to our longings.

Stormie Omartian

Heavenly Father, You are my contentment
and my peace. I find protection when I seek
Your healing hand; I discover joy when I
welcome Your healing Spirit. Let me look to
You, Lord, for the peace and contentment
that You have offered me through
the gift of Your Son.

~ Amen

My Prayer for Today

A Prayer for . . .

Knowledge of God's Will

And this world is fading away,
along with everything it craves.
But if you do the will of God,
you will live forever.

1 John 2:17 NLT

As human beings with limited understanding, we can never fully understand the will of God. But as believers in a benevolent God, we must always trust the will of our Heavenly Father.

Before His crucifixion, Jesus went to the Mount of Olives and poured out His heart to God (Luke 22). Jesus knew of the agony that He was destined to endure, but He also knew that God's will must be done. We, like our Savior, face trials that bring fear and trembling to the very depths of our souls, but like Christ, we, too, must ultimately seek God's will, not our own.

As this day unfolds, seek God's will for your own life and obey His Word. When you entrust your life to Him completely and without reservation, He will give you the strength to meet any challenge, the courage to face any trial, and the wisdom to live in His righteousness and in His peace.

If you seek to know the path of your duty,
use God as your compass.

C. H. Spurgeon

~

The purpose of all prayer is to find God's will
and to make that will our prayer.

Catherine Marshall

~

Prayer is God's provision for us to know Him,
to know His purposes and His ways,
to experience His mighty presence working
in us and through us to accomplish
His perfect will.

Henry Blackaby

~

Only God's chosen task for you will ultimately
satisfy. Do not wait until it is too late to
realize the privilege of serving Him in
His chosen position for you.

Beth Moore

Lord, let Your will be my will. When I am
confused, give me maturity and wisdom.
When I am worried, give me courage and
strength. Let me be Your faithful servant,
Father, always seeking Your guidance
and Your will for my life.

~ Amen

My Prayer for Today

My Hopes & Prayers for Next Week

My Hopes & Prayers for Next Week

Day 15
A Prayer for . . .

Priorities That Are Pleasing to God

Teach me Your way, O LORD;
I will walk in Your truth.

Psalm 86:11 NASB

"First things first." These words are easy to speak but hard to put into practice, especially for busy mothers. Why? Because so many people are tugging on mom's apron strings (either literally or figuratively).

If you're having trouble prioritizing your day, perhaps you've been trying to organize your life according to your own plans and not God's. A better strategy, of course, is to take your daily obligations and place them in the hands of the One who created you. To do so, you must prioritize your day according to God's commandments, and you must seek His will and His wisdom in all matters. Then, you can face the day with the assurance that the same God who created our universe out of nothingness will help you place first things first in your own life.

Do you feel overwhelmed or confused? Turn the concerns of this day over to a higher Source. Then, listen for His answer . . . and trust the answer He gives.

In the name of Jesus Christ who was never
in a hurry, we pray, O God, that You will
slow us down, for we know that we live
too fast. With all eternity before us, make us
take time to live—time to get acquainted
with You, time to enjoy Your blessing,
and time to know each other.

Peter Marshall

~

Blessed are those who know what on earth
they are here on earth to do and set themselves
about the business of doing it.

Max Lucado

~

The things that matter most in this world
can never be held in your hand.

Gloria Gaither

~

Aim at heaven and you will get earth
thrown in. Aim at earth
and you will get neither.

C. S. Lewis

Lord, let Your priorities be my priorities.
Let Your will be my will. Let Your Word
be my guide, and let me grow in faith
and in wisdom this day and every day.
~ Amen

My Prayer for Today

Day 16

A Prayer for . . .

A Humble Spirit

Do nothing from selfishness or empty conceit,
but with humility of mind regard one another as
more important than yourselves.

Philippians 2:3 NASB

A Prayer for . . .

As fallible human beings, we have so much to be humble about. Why, then, is humility such a difficult trait for us to master? Precisely because we are fallible human beings. Yet, if we are to grow and mature as Christians, we must strive to give credit where credit is due, starting, of course, with God and His only begotten Son.

As Christians, we have been refashioned and saved by Jesus Christ, and that salvation came not because of our own good works but because of God's grace. Thus, we are not "self-made"; we are "God-made," and we are "Christ-saved." How, then, can we be boastful? The answer, of course, is that, if we are honest with ourselves and with our God, we simply can't be boastful . . . we must, instead, be eternally grateful and exceedingly humble. Humility, however, is not easy for most of us.

All too often, we are tempted to stick out our chests and say, "Look at me; look what I did!" But, in the quiet moments when we search the depths of our own hearts, we know better. Whatever "it" is, God did that. And He deserves the credit.

God is attracted to weakness.
He can't resist those who humbly
and honestly admit how desperately
they need him.

Jim Cymbala

~

The great characteristic of the saint is humility.

Oswald Chambers

~

Humble yourselves in the sight of the Lord,
and He will lift you up.

James 4:10 NKJV

~

It was pride that changed angels into devils;
it is humility that makes men as angels.

St. Augustine

Lord, let me be a woman with a humble spirit.
Keep me mindful, Dear God, that all my gifts
come from You. When I feel prideful, remind
me that You sent Your Son to be a humble
carpenter and that Jesus was ridiculed and
crucified on a cross. Let me grow beyond my
need for earthly praise, Lord, and when I seek
approval, let me look only to You.

~ Amen

My Prayer for Today

Day 17

A Prayer for . . .

Friends

This is my commandment,
That ye love one another,
as I have loved you.

John 15:12-13 KJV

What is a friend? The dictionary defines the word *friend* as "a person who is attached to another by feelings of affection or personal regard." This definition is accurate, as far as it goes, but when we examine the deeper meaning of friendship, so many more descriptors come to mind: trustworthiness, loyalty, helpfulness, kindness, understanding, forgiveness, encouragement, humor, and cheerfulness, to mention but a few.

How wonderful are the joys of genuine friendship! Today, as you consider the many blessings that God has given you, remember to thank Him for the friends He has chosen to place along your path. May you be a blessing to them, and may they richly bless you today, tomorrow, and every day that you live.

In friendship, God opens your eyes to
the glories of Himself.

Joni Eareckson Tada

~

The best times in life are made a thousand times
better when shared with a dear friend.

Luci Swindoll

~

Nothing opens the heart but a true friend,
to whom you may impart griefs, joys,
fears, hopes, suspicions, counsels,
and whatever lies upon the heart.

Francis Bacon

~

True friends don't spend time gazing into each
other's eyes. They show great tenderness toward
each other, but they face in the same direction,
toward common projects, interest, goals,
and above all, toward a common Lord.

C. S. Lewis

Lord, thank You for my friends.
Let me be a trustworthy friend to others,
and let my love for You be reflected
in my genuine love for them.
~ Amen

My Prayer for Today

Day 18

A Prayer for . . .

Acceptance

The Lord will do what is good in his sight.
1 Chronicles 19:13 NIV

The American theologian Reinhold Niebuhr composed a profoundly simple verse that came to be known as the Serenity Prayer: "God, grant me the serenity to accept the things I cannot change, the courage to change the things I can, and the wisdom to know the difference." Niebuhr's words are far easier to recite than they are to live by. Why? Because most of us want life to unfold in accordance with our own wishes and timetables. But sometimes God has other plans.

Author Hannah Whitall Smith observed, "How changed our lives would be if we could only fly through the days on wings of surrender and trust!" These words remind us that even when we cannot understand the workings of God, we must trust Him and accept His will.

So if you've encountered unfortunate circumstances that are beyond your power to control, accept those circumstances . . . and trust God. When you do, you can be comforted in the knowledge that your Creator is both loving and wise, and that He understands His plans perfectly, even when you do not.

Acceptance is taking from God's hand
absolutely anything He gives, looking into
His face in trust and thanksgiving, knowing
that the confinement of the hedge
we're in is good and for His glory.

Charles Swindoll

～

Sometimes the greatest act of faith is
not to ask for a miracle.

Henry Blackaby

～

Part of waiting upon the Lord is telling
God that you want only what He wants—
whatever it is.

Kay Arthur

～

Trust the past to God's mercy,
the present to God's love,
and the future to God's providence.

St. Augustine

Lord, when I am discouraged, give me hope.
When I am impatient, give me peace.
When I face circumstances that I cannot
change, give me a spirit of acceptance. In all
things great and small, let me trust in You,
Dear Lord, knowing that You are the Giver
of life and the Giver of all things good,
today and forever.

~ Amen

My Prayer for Today

Day 19
A Prayer for . . .

A Worthy Testimony

For God has not given us a spirit of timidity,
but of power and love and discipline.
Therefore do not be ashamed of
the testimony of our Lord . . . .

2 Timothy 1:7-8 NASB

In his second letter to Timothy, Paul shares a message to believers of every generation when he writes, "God has not given us a spirit of timidity" (1:7 NASB). Paul's meaning is crystal clear: When sharing our testimonies, we, as Christians, must be courageous, forthright, and unashamed.

We live in a world that desperately needs the healing message of Christ Jesus. Every believer, each in his or her own way, bears a personal responsibility for sharing that message. If you are a believer in Christ, you know how He has touched your heart and changed your life. Now it's your turn to share the Good News with others. And remember: today is the perfect time to share your testimony because tomorrow may quite simply be too late.

To take up the cross means that you
take your stand for the Lord Jesus
no matter what it costs.

Billy Graham

~

Remember, a small light will do a great deal
when it is in a very dark place. Put one little
tallow candle in the middle of a large hall,
and it will give a great deal of light.

D. L. Moody

~

You cannot keep silent once you have
experienced the salvation of Jesus Christ.

Warren Wiersbe

~

God has ordained that others may see
the reality of His presence by
the illumination our lives shed forth.

Beth Moore

Dear Lord, let me share the Good News of Your Son Jesus. Let the life that I live and the words that I speak bear testimony to my faith in Him. And let me share the story of my salvation with others so that they, too, might dedicate their lives to Christ and receive His eternal gifts.

~ Amen

My Prayer for Today

A Prayer for . . .

Those Who Grieve

Blessed are those who mourn,
for they will be comforted.

Matthew 5:4 NIV

Grief visits all of us who live long and love deeply. When we lose a loved one, or when we experience any other profound loss, darkness overwhelms us for awhile, and it seems as if we cannot summon the strength to face another day—but, with God's help, we can.

When our friends or family members encounter life-shattering events, we struggle to find words that might offer them comfort and support. But finding the right words can be difficult. Sometimes, all that we can do is to be with our loved ones, offering them few words but much love.

Thankfully, God promises that He is "close to the brokenhearted" (Psalm 34:18 NIV). In times of intense sadness, we must turn to Him, and we must encourage our friends and family members to do likewise. When we do, our Father comforts us and, in time, He heals us.

There is no pit so deep that
God's love is not deeper still.

Corrie ten Boom

~

In heaven, we will see that nothing, absolutely
nothing, was wasted, and that every tear
counted and every cry was heard.

Joni Eareckson Tada

~

When all else is gone, God is still left.
Nothing changes Him.

Hannah Whitall Smith

~

God whispers to us in our pleasures,
speaks in our conscience,
but shouts in our pain.

C. S. Lewis

Lord, You have promised that You will not give us more than we can bear; You have promised to lift us out of our grief and despair; You have promised to put a new song on our lips. Today, Lord, I pray for those who mourn, and I thank You for sustaining all of us in our days of sorrow. May we trust You always and praise You forever.

~ Amen

My Prayer for Today

Day 21

A Prayer for . . .

A Thankful Heart

Give thanks in all circumstances;
for this is God's will for you in Christ Jesus.

1 Thessalonians 5:18 NIV

As believing Christians, we are blessed beyond measure. God sent His only Son to die for our sins. And, God has given us the priceless gifts of eternal love and eternal life. We, in turn, are instructed to approach our Heavenly Father with reverence and thanksgiving. But, as busy women caught up in the inevitable demands of everyday life, we sometimes fail to pause and thank our Creator for the countless blessings He has bestowed upon us.

When we slow down and express our gratitude to the One who made us, we enrich our own lives and the lives of our families and friends. Thanksgiving should become a habit, a regular part of our daily routines. Yes, God has blessed us beyond measure, and we owe Him everything, including our eternal praise.

A child of God should be a visible beatitude
for joy and a living doxology for gratitude.

C. H. Spurgeon

~

It is always possible to be thankful for what
is given rather than to complain about what
is not given. One or the other
becomes a habit of life.

Elisabeth Elliot

~

It is only with gratitude that life becomes rich.

Dietrich Bonhoeffer

~

Why wait until the fourth Thursday in
November? Why wait until the morning of
December twenty-fifth? Thanksgiving
to God should be an everyday affair.
The time to be thankful is now!

Jim Gallery

A Prayer for Today

Lord, let me be a thankful Christian.
Your blessings are priceless and eternal.
I praise You, Lord, for Your gifts and,
most of all, for Your Son. Your love endures
forever. I will offer You my heartfelt
thanksgiving this day
and throughout all eternity.
~ Amen

My Prayer for Today

My Hopes & Prayers for Next Week

My Hopes & Prayers for Next Week

Day 22
A Prayer for . . .

Spiritual Growth

But grow in the grace and knowledge of our Lord and Savior Jesus Christ. To Him be the glory, both now and to the day of eternity.

2 Peter 3:18 NASB

The journey toward spiritual maturity lasts a lifetime. As Christians, we can and should continue to grow in the love and the knowledge of our Savior as long as we live. Norman Vincent Peale had simple advice for believers of all ages: "Ask the God who made you to keep remaking you." That advice, of course, is perfectly sound but too often ignored.

When we cease to grow, either emotionally or spiritually, we do ourselves and our families a profound disservice. But, if we study God's Word, if we obey His commandments, and if we live in the center of His will, we will not be "stagnant" believers; we will, instead, be growing Christians . . . and that's exactly what God wants for our lives.

In those quiet moments when we open our hearts to God, the Creator who made us keeps remaking us. He gives us direction, perspective, wisdom, and courage. And, the appropriate moment to accept His spiritual gifts is always this one.

The vigor of our spiritual lives will be
in exact proportion to the place held by
the Bible in our lives and in our thoughts.

George Mueller

~

Do not store up for yourselves treasures on
earth, where moth and rust destroy, and where
thieves break in and steal. But store up for
yourselves treasures in heaven, where moth
and rust do not destroy, and where thieves
do not break in and steal. For where your
treasure is, there your heart will be also.

Matthew 6:19-21 NIV

~

A Christian is never in a state of completion
but always in the process of becoming.

Martin Luther

~

The maturity of a Christian experience cannot
be reached in a moment, but is the result
of the work of God's Holy Spirit, who,
by His energizing and transforming power,
causes us to grow up into Christ in all things.

Hannah Whitall Smith

A Prayer for Today

Dear Lord, when I open myself to You,
I am blessed. Let me accept Your love
and Your wisdom. Show me Your way, Lord,
and deliver me from the painful mistakes
that I make when I stray from Your
commandments. Let me live according to
Your Word, and let me grow in
my faith every day that I live.
~ Amen

My Prayer for Today

Day 23
A Prayer for . . .

Patience

It is better to be patient than powerful;
it is better to have self-control
than to conquer a city.

Proverbs 16:32 NLT

The rigors of motherhood can test the patience of the most even-tempered moms. From time to time, even the most mannerly children may do things that worry us or confuse us or anger us. Why? Because they are children, and because they are human.

As loving parents, we must be patient with our children's shortcomings (just as they, too, must be patient with our own). But our patience must not be restricted to those who live under our care. We must also strive, to the best of our abilities, to exercise patience in all our dealings because our children are watching and learning.

Sometimes, patience is simply the price we pay for being responsible parents, and that's exactly as it should be. After all, think how patient our Heavenly Father has been with us.

Patience

To receive the blessing we need, we must
believe and keep on believing, to wait
and keep on waiting. We need to wait in
prayer, wait with our Bibles open as we
confess His promises, wait in joyful praise
and worship of the God who will never
forget our case, and wait as we continue
serving others in His name.

Jim Cymbala

～

We must learn to wait.
There is grace supplied to the one who waits.

Mrs. Charles E. Cowman

～

How do you wait upon the Lord?
First you must learn to sit at His feet
and take time to listen to His words.

Kay Arthur

～

When I am dealing with an all-powerful,
all-knowing God, I, as a mere mortal,
must offer my petitions not only with
persistence but also with patience.
Someday I'll know why.

Ruth Bell Graham

A Prayer for Today

Lord, You have commanded me to choose
my words carefully so that I might be a source
of encouragement and hope to all whom I meet.
Keep me mindful, Father, that I have influence
on many people, especially my children . . .
make me an influence for good. And may
the words that I speak today be worthy
of the One who has saved me forever.

~ Amen

My Prayer for Today

Day 24
A Prayer for . . .

Obedience

Whatever you have learned or received or heard
from me, or seen in me—put it into practice.
And the God of peace will be with you.

Philippians 4:9 NIV

As loving parents, we must teach our children to obey the rules of society and the laws of God. God's laws are contained in a guidebook for righteous living called the Holy Bible. It contains thorough instructions that, if followed, lead to fulfillment, peace, righteousness, and salvation. But, if we choose to ignore God's commandments, the results are as predictable as they are tragic.

Talking about obedience is easy; living obediently is considerably harder. But, if we are to be responsible role models for our families and friends, we must study God's Word and obey it.

Phillips Brooks advised, "Be such a person, and live such a life, that if every person were such as you, and every life a life like yours, this earth would be God's Paradise." And that's sound advice because our families and friends are watching . . . and so, for that matter, is God.

Only he who believes is obedient.
Only he who is obedient believes.
Dietrich Bonhoeffer

~

Let your fellowship with the Father
and with the Lord Jesus Christ have as its one
aim and object a life of quiet, determined,
unquestioning obedience.
Andrew Murray

~

God uses ordinary people who are obedient to
Him to do extraordinary things.
John Maxwell

~

If you love Me, keep My commandments.
John 14:15 NKJV

A Prayer for Today

Dear Lord, when I obey Your commandments,
and when I trust the promises of Your Son,
I experience love, peace, and abundance.
Direct my path far from the temptations
and distractions of this world. And, let me
discover Your will and follow it,
Dear Lord, this day and always.
~ Amen

My Prayer for Today

Day 25

A Prayer for . . .

Hope

I wait quietly before God, for my hope is in him.

Psalm 62:5 NLT

Are you a hope-filled mom? You should be. After all, God is good; His love endures; and He has offered you the priceless gift of eternal life. And, of course, God has blessed you with a loving family. But sometimes, in life's darker moments, you may lose sight of those blessings, and when you do, it's easy to lose hope.

When a suffering woman sought healing by merely touching the hem of His cloak, Jesus replied, "Daughter, be of good comfort; thy faith hath made thee whole" (Matthew 9:22 KJV). The message to believers is clear: if we are to be made whole by God, we must live by faith.

If you find yourself falling into the spiritual traps of worry and discouragement, seek the healing touch of Jesus and the encouraging words of fellow Christians. This world can be a place of trials and tribulations, but as believers we are secure. Our hope is in God; He has promised us peace, joy, and eternal life. And, of course, God keeps His promises today, tomorrow, and forever. Amen!

Never yield to gloomy anticipation.
Place your hope and confidence in God.
He has no record of failure.

Mrs. Charles E. Cowman

~

Everything that is done in the world
is done by hope.

Martin Luther

~

Keep your feet on the ground, but let your heart
soar as high as it will. Refuse to be average
or to surrender to the chill of
your spiritual environment.

A. W. Tozer

~

Oh, remember this: There is never a time
when we may not hope in God. Whatever our
necessities, however great our difficulties,
and though to all appearance help is impossible,
yet our business is to hope in God,
and it will be found that it is not in vain.

George Mueller

Lord, when my heart is troubled, let me trust in You. When I become discouraged, let me depend upon You. When I lose faith in this world, let me hold tightly to my faith in You. Remind me, Dear Lord, that in every situation and in every season of life, You will love me and protect me. You are my strength, Father, and I need never lose hope because You remain sovereign today and forever.

~ Amen

My Prayer for Today

Day 26

A Prayer for . . .

A Servant's Heart

Your attitude should be the same as that of
Christ Jesus . . . taking the very nature
of a servant.

Philippians 2:5, 7 NIV

We live in a world that glorifies power, prestige, fame, and money. But the words of Jesus teach us that the most esteemed men and women in this world are not the self-congratulatory leaders of society but are instead the humblest of servants.

Today, you may feel the temptation to build yourself up in the eyes of your neighbors. Resist that temptation. Instead, serve your neighbors quietly and without fanfare. Find a need and fill it—humbly. Lend a helping hand—anonymously. Share a word of kindness—with quiet sincerity. As you go about your daily activities, remember that the Savior of all humanity made Himself a servant, and we, as His followers, must do no less.

Holy service in constant fellowship
with God is heaven below.

C. H. Spurgeon

~

Do all the good you can. By all the means
you can. In all the ways you can. In all
the places you can. At all the times you can.
To all the people you can.
As long as ever you can.

John Wesley

~

Have thy tools ready; God will find thee work.

Charles Kingsley

~

God does not do anything with us,
only through us.

Oswald Chambers

A Prayer for Today

Dear Lord, as a mother, I am an example
to every member of my family. Give me
a servant's heart and make me a faithful
steward of my gifts. Let me follow in
the footsteps of Your Son Jesus who taught us
by example that to be great in Your eyes,
Lord, is to serve others humbly,
faithfully, and lovingly.
~ Amen

My Prayer for Today

Day 27
A Prayer for . . .

A Cheerful Spirit

The cheerful heart has a continual feast.

Proverbs 15:15 NIV

On some days, as every mother knows, it's hard to be cheerful. Sometimes, as the demands of the world increase and our energy sags, we feel less like "cheering up" and more like "tearing up." But even in our darkest hours, we can turn to God, and He will give us comfort.

Few things in life are more sad, or, for that matter, more absurd, than a grumpy Christian. Christ promises us lives of abundance and joy, but He does not force His joy upon us. We must claim His joy for ourselves, and when we do, Jesus, in turn, fills our spirits with His power and His love.

How can we receive from Christ the joy that is rightfully ours? By giving Him what is rightfully His: our hearts and our souls. When we place Jesus at the center of our lives and trust Him as our personal Savior, He will transform us, not just for today but for all eternity. Then, we can share Christ's joy and His message with a world that needs both.

God is good, and heaven is forever.
And if those two facts don't cheer you up,
nothing will.

Marie T. Freeman

~

Some of us seem so anxious about
avoiding hell that we forget to celebrate
our journey toward heaven.

Philip Yancey

~

A cheerful look brings joy to the heart,
and good news gives health to the bones.

Proverbs 15:30 NIV

~

According to Jesus, it is God's will that
His children be filled with the joy of life.

Catherine Marshall

A Prayer for Today

Dear Lord, You have given me so many reasons
to celebrate. Today, let me choose an attitude of
cheerfulness. Let me be a joyful Christian, Lord,
quick to smile and slow to anger. And, let me
share Your goodness with all whom I meet
so that Your love might shine in me
and through me.

~ Amen

My Prayer for Today

Day 28

A Prayer for . . .

Moments of Silence

My soul, wait in silence for God only,
for my hope is from Him.

Psalm 62:5 NASB

The world seems to grow louder day by day, and our senses seem to be invaded at every turn. But, if we allow the distractions of a clamorous society to separate us from God's peace, we do ourselves a profound disservice. Our task, as dutiful believers, is to carve out moments of silence in a world filled with noise.

If we are to maintain righteous minds and compassionate hearts, we must take time each day for prayer and for meditation. We must make ourselves still in the presence of our Creator. We must quiet our minds and our hearts so that we might sense God's will and His love.

Has the busy pace of life robbed you of the peace that God has promised? If so, it's time to reorder your priorities and your life. Nothing is more important than the time you spend with your Heavenly Father. So be still and claim the inner peace that is found in the silent moments you spend with God. His peace is offered freely; it has been paid for in full; it is yours for the asking. So ask. And then share.

Be still, and know that I am God.

Psalm 46:10 NKJV

~

Instead of waiting for the feeling, wait upon God. You can do this by growing still and quiet, then expressing in prayer what your mind knows is true about Him, even if your heart doesn't feel it at this moment.

Shirley Dobson

~

Let this be your chief object in prayer, to realize the presence of your Heavenly Father. Let your watchword be: Alone with God.

Andrew Murray

~

Noise and words and frenzied, hectic schedules dull our senses, closing our ears to His still, small voice and making us numb to His touch.

Charles Swindoll

A Prayer for Today

Dear Lord, in the quiet moments of this day,
I will turn my thoughts and prayers to You.
In these silent moments, I will sense
Your presence, and I will seek Your will for
my life, knowing that when I accept
Your peace, I will be blessed today
and throughout eternity.
~ Amen

MY PRAYER FOR TODAY

My Hopes & Prayers for Next Week

My Hopes & Prayers for Next Week

Day 29
A Prayer for . . .

All God's Children

But if anyone causes one of these little ones
who trusts in me to lose faith, it would be better
for that person to be thrown into the sea
with a large millstone tied around the neck.

Mark 9:42 NLT

Every child is precious. Every child is unique. Every child is a priceless gift from the Creator. And, with the Father's gift comes immense responsibility. As parents, friends of parents, aunts, and grandmothers, we understand the critical importance of raising all our children with love, with discipline, and with God.

As Christians, we are commanded to care for our children . . . all of them. Let us care for our children here at home and pray for children around the world. Every child is God's child. May we, as concerned adults, behave—and pray—accordingly.

Children are not so different from kites.
Children were created to fly. But, they need
wind, the undergirding, and strength
that comes from unconditional love,
encouragement, and prayer.

Gigi Graham Tchividjian

~

Kids go where there is excitement.
They stay where there is love.

Zig Ziglar

~

Praying for our children is a noble task.
If what we are doing, in this fast-paced society,
is taking away from our prayer time for
our children, we're doing too much.

Max Lucado

~

Suffer the little children to come unto me,
and forbid them not;
for of such is the kingdom of God.

Mark 10:14 KJV

A Prayer for Today

Lord, the children of this world are
Your children. Let us love them, care for them,
nurture them, teach them, and lead them to
You. And today, as I serve as an example to
the children under my care, let my words
and deeds demonstrate the love that
I feel for them . . . and for You.
~ Amen

My Prayer for Today

Day 30

A Prayer for . . .

Love

But now abide faith, hope, love, these three;
but the greatest of these is love.

1 Corinthians 13:13 NASB

Few things in life are as precious or as enduring as a mother's love. Our mothers give us life, and they care for us. They nurture us when we are sick and encourage us when we're brokenhearted. Indeed, a mother's love is both powerful and priceless.

The words of 1st Corinthians 13 remind us that faith is important; so, too, is hope. But love is more important still. Christ showed His love for us on the cross, and, as Christians, we are called upon to return Christ's love by sharing it. Sometimes love is easy (puppies and sleeping children come to mind), and sometimes love is hard (fallible human beings come to mind). But God's Word is clear: We are to love our families and our neighbors without reservation or condition.

As a caring mother, you are not only shaping the lives of your loved ones; you are also, in a very real sense, reshaping eternity. It's a big job, a job so big, in fact, that God saw fit to entrust it to some of the most important people in His kingdom: loving moms like you.

Love

How do you spell love? When you reach
the point where the happiness, security, and
development of another person is as much of
a driving force to you as your own happiness,
security, and development, then you have
a mature love. True love is spelled G-I-V-E.
It is not based on what you can get, but rooted
in what you can give to the other person.

Josh McDowell

~

Charity says, "I grant you your rights.
I do not insist on mine. I give myself to you;
I do not insist that you give yourself to me."

Elisabeth Elliot

~

He who is filled with love is filled
with God Himself.

St. Augustine

~

It is important to know that you have to work
to keep love alive; you have to protect it
and maintain it, just like you would
a delicate flower.

James Dobson

A Prayer for Today

Dear Lord, You have blessed me
and my family with a love that is infinite
and eternal. May we love You more and more
each day. Make me a worthy parent
and a loving servant. And, let me show
my love for You, Lord, by sharing Your message
and Your love with my family
and with the world.

~ Amen

My Prayer for Today

Day 31
A Prayer for . . .

Salvation

For God so loved the world that he gave
his one and only Son, that whoever believes in
him shall not perish but have eternal life.

John 3:16 NIV

How marvelous it is that God became a man and walked among us. Had He not chosen to do so, we might feel removed from a distant Creator. But ours is not a distant God. Ours is a God who understands—far better than we ever could—the essence of what it means to be human.

God understands our hopes, our fears, and our temptations. He understands what it means to be angry and what it costs to forgive. He knows the heart, the conscience, and the soul of every person who has ever lived, including you. And God has a plan of salvation that is intended for you. Accept it. Accept God's gift through the person of His Son Christ Jesus, and then rest assured: God walked among us so that you might have eternal life; amazing though it may seem, He did it for you.

Before a man can be saved, he must feel
a consuming spiritual hunger. Where a hungry
heart is found, we may be sure that
God was there first.

A. W. Tozer

~

God is always ready to meet people
wherever they are, no matter how dreadful
their sins may seem.

Jim Cymbala

~

The supreme force in salvation is God's grace.
Not our works. Not our talents.
Not our feelings. Not our strength.

Max Lucado

~

The way to be saved is not to delay,
but to come and take.

D. L. Moody

A Prayer for Today

Dear Lord, I am only here on this earth for
a brief while. But, You have offered me
the priceless gift of eternal life through
Your Son Jesus. I accept Your gift, Lord,
with thanksgiving and praise. Let me share
the Good News of my salvation with
all those who need Your healing touch.
~ Amen

My Prayer for Today

My Hopes & Prayers for Next Month

My Hopes & Prayers for Next Month

My Hopes & Prayers for Next Month

My Hopes & Prayers for Next Month

Selected
Scripture

Worry

Don't worry about anything; instead,
pray about everything. Tell God what you need,
and thank him for all he has done.

Philippians 4:6 NLT

~

For this reason I say to you, do not be worried
about your life, as to what you will eat
or what you will drink; nor for your body, as to
what you will put on. Is not life more than food,
and the body more than clothing? Look at
the birds of the air, that they do not sow, nor
reap nor gather into barns, and yet
your heavenly Father feeds them.
Are you not worth much more than they?

Matthew 6:25-26 HCSB

~

Trust in him at all times, O people;
pour out your hearts to him,
for God is our refuge.

Psalm 62:8 NIV

Let not your heart be troubled;
you believe in God,
believe also in Me.

~

John 14:1 NKJV

Miracles

You are the God who performs miracles; you display your power among the peoples.

Psalm 77:14 NIV

~

God verified the message by signs and wonders and various miracles and by giving gifts of the Holy Spirit whenever he chose to do so.

Hebrews 2:4 NLT

~

Jesus said to them, "I have shown you many great miracles from the Father."

John 10:32 NIV

~

That is what the Scriptures mean when they say, "No eye has seen, no ear has heard, and no mind has imagined what God has prepared for those who love him."

1 Corinthians 2:9 NLT

For with God nothing
shall be impossible.

~

Luke 1:37 KJV

Behavior

Even a child is known by his actions,
by whether his conduct is pure and right.

Proverbs 20:11 NIV

~

Therefore, get your minds ready for action,
being self-disciplined, and set your hope
completely on the grace to be brought
to you at the revelation of Jesus Christ.
As obedient children, do not be conformed
to the desires of your former ignorance but,
as the One who called you is holy,
you also are to be holy in all your conduct.

1 Peter 1:13-15 HCSB

~

A good person produces good deeds from
a good heart, and an evil person produces
evil deeds from an evil heart.
Whatever is in your heart
determines what you say.

Luke 6:45 NLT

You see that a person is justified
by what he does
and not by faith alone.

~

James 2:24 NIV

Anger

All bitterness, anger and wrath, insult and
slander must be removed from you, along with
all wickedness. And be kind and compassionate
to one another, forgiving one another,
just as God also forgave you in Christ.
Ephesians 4:31-32 HCSB

～

I want men everywhere to lift up holy hands
in prayer, without anger or disputing.
1 Timothy 2:8 NIV

～

If anyone considers himself religious and
yet does not keep a tight rein on his tongue,
he deceives himself and his religion is worthless.
James 1:26 NIV

～

For God hath not appointed us to wrath,
but to obtain salvation
by our Lord Jesus Christ . . . .
1 Thessalonians 5:9 KJV

A fool gives full vent
to his anger, but a wise man
keeps himself under control.

~

Proverbs 29:11 NIV

Children

Fix these words of mine in your hearts
and minds. Teach them to your children,
talking about them when you sit at home
and when you walk along the road,
when you lie down and when you get up.

Deuteronomy 11:18-19 NIV

~

Train up a child in the way he should go,
and when he is old he will not depart from it.

Proverbs 22:6 NKJV

~

Then He took a child, had him stand among
them, and taking him in His arms, He said
to them, "Whoever welcomes one little child
such as this in My name welcomes Me.
And whoever welcomes Me does not
welcome Me, but Him who sent Me."

Mark 9:36-37 HCSB

Let the little children
come to Me; don't stop them,
for the kingdom of God
belongs to such as these.

~

Mark 10:14 HCSB